DUMP
TRUCKS
HAUL!

by Beth Bence Reinke

BUMBA BOOKS™

LERNER PUBLICATIONS ◆ MINNEAPOLIS

Note to Educators:

Throughout this book, you'll find critical thinking questions. These can be used to engage young readers in thinking critically about the topic and in using the text and photos to do so.

Lerner Publications Company
A division of Lerner Publishing Group, Inc.
241 First Avenue North
Minneapolis, MN 55401 USA

For reading levels and more information, look up this title at www.lernerbooks.com.

Library of Congress Cataloging-in-Publication Data

Names: Reinke, Beth Bence, author.
Title: Dump trucks haul! / by Beth Bence Reinke.
Description: Minneapolis : Lerner Publications, 2017. | Includes bibliographical references and index.
Identifiers: LCCN 2016039578 (print) | LCCN 2016045520 (ebook) | ISBN 9781512433593 (lb : alk. paper) | ISBN
    9781512455434 (pb : alk. paper) | ISBN 9781512450231 (eb pdf)
Subjects: LCSH: Dump trucks—Juvenile literature.
Classification: LCC TL230.15 .R44 2017 (print) | LCC TL230.15 (ebook) | DDC 629.224—dc23

LC record available at https://lccn.loc.gov/2016039578

Manufactured in the United States of America
1—CG—7/15/17

Expand learning beyond the printed book. Download free, complementary educational resources for this book from our website, www.lernerresource.com.

Table of
Contents

Dump Trucks

Dump trucks are big machines.

They carry and dump heavy loads.

People use dump trucks

at construction sites.

They move dirt and rocks.

Where else could a dump truck be useful?

The cab is at the front

of the dump truck.

The driver sits in the cab.

The bed is at the back.

The bed holds the load.

Construction vehicles
work together.
An excavator fills the
dump truck bed with dirt.
The dump truck drives
the dirt away.

The bed tips up.

The dirt slides out.

It fills a hole.

Why does

the bed tip?

A front loader drops dirt

in the bed.

The dump truck takes

the dirt to another site.

**What could dirt
help build?**

The biggest dump trucks work

at mines.

The driver climbs a ladder to the cab.

Big dump trucks from mines are wide.

They are too big to drive on roads.

The tires are as tall as two men.

Dump trucks haul

load after load.

They help workers

do big jobs.

Parts of a Dump Truck

bed

cab

tire

Picture Glossary

construction sites

places where construction, or building, takes place

excavator

a large machine that scoops

front loader

a vehicle with a large scoop in the front that is used for digging and loading

mines

pits where machines dig up rocks

23

Read More

Hayes, Amy. *Big Dump Trucks*. New York: Cavendish Square Publishing, 2016.

Jango-Cohen, Judith. *Dump Trucks on the Move*. Minneapolis: Lerner Publications, 2011.

Oachs, Emily Rose. *Dump Trucks*. Minneapolis: Bellwether Media, 2017.

Index

Photo Credits